Midnight M

CW00486588

Poetry

Journey into a midnight world of music.
Euphoria and memories at midnight, dancing to
electronic music.
A love song to the sounds, beats, rhythms, symphonies,
and melodies
that make me feel more than alive.

For the music that made me feel the magic
And for all those unforgettable nights

let us light the candles in our mind
maybe we'll find something we left behind
speak in Latin, speak in code
as long as the voice is from your soul
hidden castles in the clouds
paintings moving in your town
it was never about them anyway
it's your game so play how you play

attracted to your light
shot like a beam,
I didn't put up a fight
attracted to your dark
because we all know,
that's how you see the spark

you asked me once
to describe how I'm feeling
and I played you a song
because I've always been
better at putting words
into poetry and music
as an accurate representation
of the stirrings in my soul

the sound of your rhythmic beat
in my mind tastes so sweet
deeper waters flowing like a symphony
in you, lives a constructed harmony
you created your world by design
just like the way I've curated mine
so tonight we met on purpose
a glitch in the circuit
a vocal chorus

we're deep in the heart of darkness
what's written beneath the surface
what are you willing to risk and lose
what are you willing to become, you choose

the serendipitous winds are blowing my way
silent footsteps walk from night into day
I'll build a bonfire and burn brighter than before
and the trust in myself, I will restore

scent of midnight candles burning bright
citrus leaves, wild berry flames in the night
encased in the liberating essence of change
it's all on you to choose your way
delightful musk's of hard truths and honesty
I'll burn the candles throughout this odyssey
courage to realise I've got a long way to go
a student of life, like a flower, I'll grow

it all starts as an idea, a thought in your mind
everything plays off everything else
you get out of it what you put in
you know what to do in order to win

out in the wild
nature's smile
skie's sweet kiss
nothing beats this
there's music in
everything around you
the owls hum a tune
nature's song

you played my heart strings like a harp on my soul
brushing your fingertips along my bones
yours is the only touch I want to feel for eternity
kisses and music, and you and me

when my own world was imploding, all unbound
I found reverie in nature's sound
at night, I'd sneak away into the woods,
musical misfits had brought the goods
vibrations of beats fly out the speakers
one note and I knew these nights would be sleepless
following the sound of beating hearts
that's when the serotonin release starts
amongst others who call this place home
alive in the night, alive in the sound, that's what I know
dancing like this moment would last forever
so much love for those nights, the euphoria
my soul would heal like it was a real trick
ecstatic ecstasy forever in the midnight music

many more conversations I wish I'd had with you
if it had played out another way,
now I write poetry and let the rhymes sing true
in prettier words what I wanted to say

I'd always gone against the grain
something in me shivered at being the same
the smoky mist that visited me in daydreams
was my own kiss of life against the mainstream
no, I'm a river flowing deeper than the majority
different waters, an anomaly

new year's eve would come around on the chime
I wonder what you were doing, while I was celebrating
mine
a young girl that would sneak out amidst the crackles of
sparklers and champagne pops
to steal a moment for herself before the starlight
resolutions drop
wandering the roads, making promises to her future
heart
she's made writing stories the most beautiful art

what hieroglyphics had you etched on me
an inscription for you to read, some cryptic graffiti

lost with you in the electronic trance
with you I always loved the dance

you were such an incredible inspirational instrumental
the sound of it all is elemental
in the dead of night,
I'd never felt more alive
vigorous energy flowing effortlessly, endlessly
getting caught up in your world recklessly
indescribable musical ecstasy

those nights changed my soul alchemically
the music always running through me, electrically

words became her weapon of choice
finding again her beautiful voice
and she wielded them as sharp as a pirate wields a blade
telling stories, testifying her life that she has made
deep as the roots that run under the woods
and her words can cut into places steel never could

a beauty, a transcendent girl
music touches her soul
like nothing else in this world

the music in her mind is a constant sound
consistently playing all the time
she has a heartbeat of a champion
not just for show
she's a performer in life
but some things you can't fake
and she's never had to pretend this
it's as natural as the stars shining at night

her eternal music
otherworldly magic
that slipped through
into her heart
and on her tongue

I heard a song in my dream
dripping from the starlight stream
it was my definition of a successful symphony
and I woke with crystal clear clarity
a vision of where I'm going
to tell you the truth I've always felt a knowing
a feeling inside to run with my mind
trust my gut and I saw my soul smile
always playing my song
and so the story goes on

reload the barrel and shoot the gun
darling in your head you've already won
potent potential stirring inside your heart
re-evaluate, revive and ignite the spark

with you it was more than real
what your soul made mine feel

you allowed me to see the things in me
tiny cracks I'd tried to cover with night's musical beat
being with you, made me see the hurt in my heart
fractures not reconciled, not by far
and the good times were once in a lifetimes
but the bad times felt like psychological crimes
I have to heal my own wounds that run deep
before I can rest, before I can sleep
so much alike in so many ways
a lot of things were hard to say
haunted by the memories of our love
I had fallen for you with just one look
it hurts to think about the night we met
this wound in my heart is still so fresh
you were everything I needed and more
soul touching the love I bore
your caress of my mind, your touch on my skin
your shining eyes, your grin
the way you'd look at me, I swear I'd see my soul
I suppose now our love will never grow old
I'll remember us young and alive always
a fiery love, burning ablaze
everywhere I go I see your name
excruciating and euphoric connection, twin flame

I was propelling myself forward into my new life
because if I look back, I will die

I never fit in with the girls in the castle wanting an easy
run
my life would be an adventure of doing what needs to be
done
how well can I play the game
ever-changing, never the same
what riches can I unlock, infinite levels, a world to
explore
within myself beats a well of something more
I could never be a normal one
and knowingly set off the decay in my soul
why would I unto myself become a liar
when I can walk in my truth and set my soul on fire

do you hear me dear heart,
alone in the sea of stars
my voice is trembling, but I'll still sing
remember the sound of my wings
to say what I have to say
I'll always find a way

what if I said this is a poetic journal entwined
a musical blueprint for the minds so inclined
to understand the artistic way to explain
and perceive the laws in the game
the recipe for success whispering in poetry
decorated and delivered so sweetly
for those who in their soul know
and want more than just a pretty poem

you thought it was over
you'd forgotten how to dream
but it's never over when
you're a glitch in the machine

she found her courage
to rebuild her garden

picturing what I could be
the hope, the love it gave me
a brighter goal
another transformation of the art in my soul

the quiet town of your mind
where all could happen
memories you will find
portraits of your former self form a pattern
breathe life into the chambers of your heart and head
do as you do and do as you've said
with all your heart, you know you can
every great victory starts with a plan

you could not tear my eyes away from her and I wasn't
afraid to show it
dripping in imperial stardust, encased in music, the
creative poet

a world unto herself

beautiful serenity, deliberate integrity
butterflies and flowers, mighty prosperity

I knew it when I walked away from you that day, I felt it
even with all the pain and the sadness
I knew deep inside me
this would be the turning point of my life
this would be the beginning of a new me
such a strange feeling to feel both pain and euphoria all
at once

pyre's of forgotten things,
fly on dragon wings
brightly shines the night
when she sits down to write
the world hears her think
the stars are all she drinks

you had become self-taught
tell me when did you become afraid of your own
thoughts
you know you're made with a different light
feed your flames with your truth and burn bright

her imperial nature
she's a bona fide
real one

I toil away at midnight writing poetry
because the best thoughts come to me
in the midnight hours when the stars sing
and the whispers are all but shouting
they find me in the hours before dawn
and ideas ignite and creation is born

I can feel the essence of me again
my life force, I will sustain

I knew it was all in my mind
the stories of once upon a time

what does your own
train of thought look like
and where does it go

an anthem in my heart
a voice with a higher pitch
raising the frequency
to live on higher levels

come and play with the voices in your mind
listen to what they have to say
in the hurt, I had to change
I've found the real price of progress is pain

I'm moving in a new way
falling in love with the journey

perspective darling- lift your gaze
train your mind with every thought
your brain is a like a computer
programme it well

the order of the day dissolves
when the stars shine in their numbers
I have that one star and she knows what I talk of
a symbol of her authenticity painted in the stars

down a lonely road at midnight
I walk alone with a beating heart
street signs light up the way
along with the stars dew

there's no more time and energy for deflection
now it's painful for that inner reflection
got to change my ways before it's too late
become so undeniable, there's no debate

I hold the power, the only one
I'm who I am today because of what I've done
go through the pain, a pirate on treasure island
out of the flames of suffering I forged a diamond
from under the clouds so bleak and gloomy
I became my own sunlight and shone like a ruby
and just like in the legends of old
I turned myself from dust into gold

there are others
who hear the wild
in them and smile

I began to look at it all differently
and found in science and art, poetry

play the energy like you play a piano
feel the synth waves in the air
touch them like a dance
of particles moving everywhere
until you operate so in tune
with the energy in your heart

how well do you know the river flowing in you
feel the current, no one has got your back like you do
so move and conduct in a way that matches your vision
you're the only one who needs to understand your
mission

that night I
sat in my car
looking at a city
of a sea of
shimmering lights
and realised
they were all halogen
and I was fluorescent
time to move city
and be around the
creative minds
that are made from
the same light

once I started doing what I want to do
I saw the signs in the machine everywhere
neon lights talking to me
my favourite numbers everywhere I turn
when I trusted the universe, it trusted me back
and I learnt to trust myself again

her shining authenticity
a woman of prodigious perspicacity
she's a rogue, never conforming to the status quo
she's a dreamer with a plan, a mind in the know
she's a woman with starlight energy
bright heart, her own remedy

I left in the dead of night
while the others slept
and walked across the bridge
into my new life
and was met with a
pink sunrise
and the warm feeling
of being true to my soul

there was a great rediscovery in her
as she remembered the conversations
she used to have with herself
and the conversations she has now
she realised in her renewal
how much energy
she was giving away for so long
now she's back and she's learnt a lot
and her mind is no longer an enemy
but her closest friend

and that day I rose with the sun
and I walked into the forest
the first rays of light and small warmth
from the sun, felt like kisses on my cheek
there's so much life in me still
I knew I was going to be
a force to be reckoned with

never settle with average
when starlight exists

I want to push to my potential
and feel the stardust rub together
with the blood in my veins
for every moment of life
I'm being all that I can be

until the voices inside me
become a battle cry

as I walked through the forest
I had grown up walking in
I looked through the eyes
of my younger self
and saw what I imagined
the world to be
how I wanted my world to be
and that was a gift
for the trees in that forest
had watched me grow
and held memories
and part of my essence
I'm friends with them all
and I tell them stories
and they know me
as the girl with
blonde hair and green eyes
and a story in her heart

the greatest poetess of all time
with a repertoire of words
and meaning and phrases
pulsating in her mind
the only things she consumes
are stories, prose, and poems

what happens when fiction
crosses into the realms of reality
I write a book that's steeped in fantasy
but it doesn't mean it's not true

I'm awake at night, relighting the candles inside me

she's starting to
understand how it works
everything is poetry
including herself
and the woman
she is becoming

now is the time for lions to roar

if I allowed myself to be broken
I would remember the words left unspoken
because I danced with the flame's energy in the song
ripped my heart open to find what was there all along
a beat in my soul, a rhythm playing on
the music that filled where there once was none

thought of a twin flame
burning in my mind

when they dipped his soul into the cosmic dust
they must have dipped it twice into the starry stream
for he speaks with a different tongue
and looks with different eyes
I understand him effortlessly
and I welcome what he has to say
for it is in my mind also

candlesticks and magical things
pumpkins glowing on owl wings
welcoming bonfire season with red and fallen leaves
your beauty wanes and wakes in autumn thieves
planting the seeds, sowing in the deep
come spring, your harvest you will reap

find what was buried under silent things
where music comes alive and shakes it's wings

for in this world, where nothing is as it seems
you walk in the shadows of the light in dreams
night is falling, someone's sending out the flares
brave of heart, you seek and you dare
come and glimpse the meaning of eternity
for you, it was an instant affinity

shake off the old, you don't need it anymore
cast off the death at autumn's door
welcome the new, the lantern unknown
carry it down the paths unsown
ghosts in the system, wandering eyes
tell me a tale and the story flies
I'll light a fire and make it brighter
it's in my blood, a poet, a writer

set up like you've already won
I'll bet on me,
I'll do what needs to be done

on this Halloween night
I'll carve the pumpkins
in the shape of a heart
for I've always loved
the ghost stories
that make your
heart beat
a little faster

a journey by candlelight in the lamp lit streets
the chill in the air, strangers and lovers meet
I carry nothing but the light in my soul
another one to etch on the scroll

the cauldrons bubbling, the batch is brew
I added a drop of my heart fire to make it true
along with sage and a cat's insight into the spiritual
drops of desire and clear headedness from my daily
ritual
inhale the magic from the smoke and drink all the potion
taste the courage in my soul, alive and never broken

a deep dive into dream state and imagination
ideas and thoughts that warrant illumination
run with the wild wolf inside
you didn't come this far for the spark to die

I carry that candle and keep it aflame
in it's lights I've written my name
there is magic for those who seek it
you know it girl, you're the wild spirit

revival of epic proportion
she's as true as they come, no distortion
oh her music is always on key
dancing in twilight's river, ever so free

colours of the stream
winds in the milky way
I'll ride a star with the witches tonight
drunk on endless starlight
don't let your dream die
as long as your heart beats, control your mind
imagine it all, and come alive
see how you run, see how you fly

lovers without names
lost in the flames
I love the burn

you kiss the stars every night
on the road to your heart
a renewal of your mind, everything you know is yours
claim the magic in your soul and watch your spirit soar

sunset of pink and gold
a story I've watched in my head but never told
whispers of enchanting things stir in my soul
did you hear the song of the wolves

down these halls I've composed my symphony
playing on the piano a song, a melody
my tears and soul light have forged this euphony
star-lit lyrics, enrapturing harmony

the wild wolves in my soul run free
as phantoms on the wind echo voices to me
can you touch the waves in the air
lightning strikes on the one who's soul is rare

storms hail down with thunder's sound
don't turn back now, stand your ground

midnight echoes, woods alive
fairy pools, souls revive
wandering foots, turquoise fireflies
stars illuminate the way
what stirs here, you won't find in the day
gnomes playing by the water
I know it now, I'm night's daughter
for it is the dark between the stars
that have seen my hidden scars
I keep them tucked away in the light
but I can't hide my soul from the night

night black wolves in my dreams
lead me to starlight streams

an invitation to a Halloween ball
ghosts and ghouls haunt the hall
come sit by the fire's hearth
we're telling stories of our journeys,
of the courage in our hearts
that lead us to something greater
and how not to become ghosts of ourselves
as we journey onwards to our dreams

if it's a game she has played
she finally took off the masquerade
unburdened herself from what had become heavy
treads lightly, this game is deadly
she knows the cards she has at hand
her dreams come flesh and take a stand

a soul in need of renewal, welcomes autumn's change
as the leaves fall, so does the bird break free from the
cage
it's a bitter pill to swallow when you realise
you were the captor holding yourself in chains
knowingly or unknowingly, it doesn't matter
free yourself now, and the prison of your mind, shatter
it was only you in your way all along
now bloom little bird, play your bird song

pumpkin pies and apple strudel
wellies walking in leafy puddles
hot herbal teas and one put stews
auburn leaves, all is new
abandoned castles, and abbey ruins
autumn life begins
walks on roads in the forest's hue
halfway to everywhere, dreams come true
a cosy coat to keep me warm
nights that last long to welcome the dawn
camping in a meadow under the sky
reading books that make me cry
it's like the autumn flames enchant the world
and inspire the beauty of that girl

pink fire of dusk on the sky's face
cracks of leaves in the darkness
hidden streets, time to trespass
I'll never be like you
I make my own rules

railroads covered in orange foliage
train tracks that lead to everywhere
magical journeys

wooden stairways in the forest's glow
a tea party in the woods
eating cake and talking of plans
scheming plots
whispers into the night
comrades gather to talk of revolution
a revolt of rebels in a mastermind

singing in the old ruins by the lake
a monastery of hearts
beating for the song inside

a heart on fire shakes its wings
and blooms

she drinks maple syrup
and berry juice
mixed with the water
of the stars
always a sweet tooth
and a sweetheart

a starlit journey
through mountain peaks
on a train for untamed spirits

I'm a creature of the night at my core
but now I've started to wake up and greet the sunrise
because each day I watch the darkness turn into light
brings me hope for a new dawn, a new fight to fight
so I wake before the birds tweet
while souls are in lullaby sleep
does the world stir in the witching hour
I rise up and leave my humble abode
out in the darkness I travel into nature
and walk up the mountain
to greet the blazing light
and be grateful for the new day
infinite potential all the way

writing a story
I carry the characters in my mind
so understand that
before I can write a story
I must first become one

the cat watched me walk alone
across the road heading to the forest
at this time in the early hours
before the sunrise
it was just him and I, awake
beginning to think the thoughts we think

I told you that night, I told you the truth
in the tingling of my soul, it was always you

lit the match of a thousand flowers, a battle won
now you are beautiful, strong you have become

for the heartbeat of the world
is heard by a creative girl
a nod from the universe
bright and luminous
a sign in the star's sea
to pursue with all her heart, her journey

imagination is home
stories have a home in me

to the woman I am becoming,
optimize your internal assets
and operate like a champion
in everything you do
move like starry water
run like a wolf
fly like a butterfly

it feels like flames
igniting in my veins
now I'm moving
in the direction
that my soul sings
to spread my wings

darling, never neglect the power you have
to at any moment decide you want different
and begin acting accordingly to your desires

she moved differently to before
concentrating all her energy
into the song she's composing
with every moment and every breath

the feeling of constantly improving
and seeing your results bloom
like a wildfire
is more addicting than any drug
you could self-subscribe

only those who are willing
to find out what they are made of
and see how far the well goes
are going to taste the sweetness
of what life truly has to offer

she understands the language of the universe
she hears the music on the waves of life
every night she plays her soul song
and converses with the mysteries of the cosmos
and of her own heart

come you dreamers, misfits and rogues
hold the mirror up to your own soul
you've got the mind to go all in
move out of your own way and you'll win

she paints a picture
of the castle in her head
building an empire of
ideas and plans
and action
until she shoots
an arrow
that never misses
her target

the ones who don't belong
what to feel when the love is gone
is there anything left of you
you've played the part for so long
I know I'll find what is true
my truth is written in a song
in midnight's music it came alive
that celestial fire buried inside

she masters her craft with the art in her soul
delicate yet as strong as her heart strings
that will never break
and that make the sweetest music

it feels like the crushing of waves down upon you
it feels like a storm all around you
but you will learn that this will make you stronger
and when lightning and thunder come knocking again
you will smile because you have your own

her mental capacity
her natural ferocity
her intellectual capabilities
her ability to adapt, elasticities
her lightning blood, electricity
her mind on fire with an electric flame
a glitch, the name of the game

as I live more of my life
I realise the only thing
I know for sure
is that writing poetry
makes me feel alive

I was young and drank fool's potion every night
I thought I knew all the world's secrets and then some
but now when change is in my armoury
I realise just how foolish I was to search the world
before I had uncovered and charted myself

the creative process
is as mysterious as imagination
who do I have to become
to channel and capture
the energy of thoughts
I want to be thinking
so the words will
come pouring out
like a ribbon of light

it must mean something
if that beating heart of mine
feels like it's beating in tune
with the rhythm of the universe
when I pick up a pen
and write from the ink in my soul

teal starlight, wondrous lightning
dance with thunder in my heart
a force of nature, energy of the stars

she knew filling her own stream
with the stars in her heart
would yield a brighter vitality
for her life

a journey through your mind
and we stopped at an inn
for warmth and shelter
and met the bard who sang a song

tell me a story girl
with infinite stories
inside her soul

I'll never forget the story
the words are etched on my soul print
embedded in the starlight in my heart

you take the journey
not for the destination
but for the transformation
for who you become

I dreamt of you last night
your touch as real as life
I'll always love you
I know that to be true
parts of me in you and you in me
hearts connected by a golden string
we will meet again in this game
drawn back to each other, twin flame

our stories are so entwined
it's like you had dipped
your pen in my soul ink
to write these pages

her soul is pulsating
with electric stars
an energy so rare
you won't come
across it again
in your lifetime

the sweetest drink is
who you are becoming

I've tasted of some potions
and felt the connection of the world
the network of vibrations and frequency
and of my own energy in my body
a combination spiritual and physical
and the infinite potential of what I could be

what if Elysium
is a state of mind

perspective of a mind
that feeds on starlight
if you don't like the story
collect the information
and change the narrative
you're the writer

she has a rich mind
bottled bravery
tinctures of solutions
cups of wisdom
water always flowing
never stagnant
electricity surging
creating new networks
in her brain
that's how she wins

the glitch in the game
your song is not the same

I've met you before in the astral realm
it was inevitable we would meet in the game
once I'd levelled up my character
playing at a higher calibre

the candles on the walls
whispering forgotten things
the light of the setting sun
illuminating her wings

a new woman that she can't hide
darling welcome to the turning tide
so focused on the alchemy of herself
blocking out all other noises
her transformation is her resolution
this is the revolution

a candle in the shape of a star
with smoke rising with butterfly wings
from the chimney of her home
burning tales of yesteryear on the fire

there's a certain freedom in movement
in the art of dancing through life
in caressing your own power
as you continuously move forward
and decide what move to make next

I thought no one but me
heard the song of the stars
until I heard the humming in your heart

by my own definition of success
I will choose the scent of oil for me
and light a match to set fire to my soul

the best thing about having
all these dreams as a young girl
is becoming a woman
who makes them come true

like a firework
you have to go
all the way into yourself
deeper and deeper
and pull from
the infinite well
feed the air and fire
and combust and explode

sun dancer
star painter
story writer

she's of a different calibre
a starlight heart
beating to a cosmic sound

she's the ruler of her own mind
a sorceress of energy
enchantress to herself
the rarest anomaly

the whispers of the
willow tree
vines like my veins
pathways of light
where ideas surge
like electric sparks
in a circuit in my mind

she's the storm bringer
world dweller
lightning wielder
star dancer
poetry dreamer
imagination creator

the girl with the sparkling eyes
out in the night as the stars fly
what's on your mind, girl made of stories
analysing your losses and your glories
a strategic battle planner, always thinking
from her own waters, she is drinking
just like the stars, always twinkling
she's knows to win in this game
she must first win in her mind
burn with that turquoise flame
a girl of a different kind

she fly's
like wild blooms
and shows
her colourful
feathers
a nightingale
with
starlit wings

a network
of the highest
frequency
mind on fire
soul alive

your next venture into the unknown
walking into the horizon all on your own
surely the travellers whispered of desire
the best way to forge your path is through fire

romance at dawn
passion at dusk

the girl with the star tattoo
shines with her truth
some things are innate
and can't be taught
I will be the one to dictate
the energy of my thoughts

sailing the seven seas, pirates' gold
rare as soul dust in legends old
treasure of the elusive one
what if the real prize is a mind of freedom

she made herself with stars and fire
she created herself through music and light
she built herself on courage and truth
she constructed herself at noon and midnight
she educated herself with real knowledge
and she knows she is the designer and the architect
of who she is and who she will become

two hearts meeting
it was alchemical

the glitches are starting to rise
the ones who see the world with real eyes

no more thought pollution
wanderers of the night
spark the revolution

rebel with a cause
we make the laws
making moves consciously
welcome to the odyssey

write it down like the Tabellion
make a note, here comes the rebellion

it's been simmering in the cauldron
the innate feeling to be the master
of your own soul
maestro to your own song

it all starts
when you decide
to take responsibility
of your own soul

it was just a whisper
we would talk at night
an idea turned to a plan
and action takes flight

burning with the midnight flame
always changing, never the same

music in her
dripping in notes of potential
about to be composed
into masterpieces
symphonies
blissfully playing
from the instrument
in her soul

that moment felt like eternity
musical memory of you and me

sing my soul a lullaby

she is the ultimate instrument
playing her song
and tuning the music
to create the reality
she sees in her mind

it's always been about
listening to the music in your soul
and playing louder than the noise outside
and performing better than you did before

it's written like the stars of once upon a time
code or any language, make it rhyme
runaway to join the night
potions make stars take flight

a gypsy woman to tell my fortune
under the illuminating moon
show your dark side
deep and mysterious, there's nothing to hide
go through phases like the everchanging tide
shine with the light in the waters
if anything, heartbreak has taught us
pain is inevitable, so wear it like you could stand it longer
after all who would you be, if the loss hadn't made you
stronger

meet me at the crossroads
bring your grand piano
and we'll play a tune
and hum a song
till the sunlight's piercing arrow

he smiled at her
with his midnight blue eyes
there's no going back now
you know too much

the depth of her desire
far surpassed any daydream
so clearly is the vision in her mind
a calculated, evaluated plan
carefully thought-out extraction
no distraction
she's on a quest to win

with him I belong
I know it in my bones
I know it in my soul

didn't they tell you
a warrior's heart beats differently
and one knows the sound of another

you're a different breed
it's written all over your face
you're a magnetic song
compelling in all aspects
in a class of your own
a wonder in this world
of average hearts
but my darling
no one would ever
mistake you
for any less than
a girl glowing with stars

play the ballad of broken hearts
cheer for the mental agony
for the pain is the beginning
of a new and brighter birth

she's a butterfly on fire
with her deepest desires
success is her only option

her night long laments for herself
left her with the epiphany
that she was not being all she could be
and so she entered the new state of mind
and shone with the light of a brighter kind

I knew I could trust you straight away
that visceral reaction doesn't lie

what if the most beautiful sound
is your beating heart
when you decide to follow it

how could I mistake the passion in your eyes
for anything other than the turquoise fire inside

building a relationship
with my imagination
repairing old fractures
deep cuts buried inside
scars in my mind
thinking of all I can be
just my mind and me

a beat of music
a sea of strangers
faces become a blur
it's all the same
but seeing you
something changed

it's like the music in my mind changed tune
and a melody burst at the sight of you
who knows to what part of the cosmos that night went
but all the humming's in my mind made sense

wild as the fox, free as the sea
living like twilight, endlessly

welcome Mr conductor to the order of play
you used to control the rhythm
but now the instruments are in my hands
I'm taking back the beat now
and so the music plays on

no matter what they say
always play it your way

constantly evolving with who I am
stagnant water is poison
but moving water is life

bright blue eyes
watching the sunrise
you are told a thousand lies
but the truth is always brought to light

fruits are nature's sweets
grapes on the vine
taste like a sip of the divine

midnight witches
with their emerald energy
know how to cast spells
with their words and poetry

she thought she knew
but the world changes
as her perspective does
perception is everything
how you look at the world matters

hearing music
that has never
been played before

music's soul came alive
in those sunlight butterflies

I'd never given anyone
the power to break
my heart before
until I met you
and I was sure
the moment we met
I knew you had it
in your hands
and I had yours

to tell you the truth
no one had ever connected
with my soul like yours
I'd had my fair share
of eyes to look into
but none looked back
into mine the way
yours did
so I'll write it hear
in case we
never cross paths
once more
I know in my soul
you're like no other
your shine is rare
I recognised it at first glance
I knew I'd met you before
our hearts had loved,
our souls had danced
I wish you well on your quest
and with the workings of the world
I have a feeling we will meet again

the only company I'll keep
are the ones in love with their fire
the mad ones who think differently
the ones dancing with their song

how you decide to live
is entirely up to you darling

olive trees under the Greek sun
philosophers of ancient times
singing a song
the pioneers sung
hum in the rocks
rhythm in the sand
pilgrimage across deserts
a journey begun

I'm starting to love the journey

footprints in the woods
a quiet spirit walked beside me
maybe it was my future self
and maybe it's the ghosts of the
stoics that have come before
leaving signs that the way is
possible and attainable

the most devastating thing is
I must have been so out of tune with myself
in those moments with you
I realise now, it's not your fault, it's mine
flashbacks in pain, it hurts to remember
lessons learned, not repeated
the thoughts of it are nightmares
but I know I will never do that to myself again
now to move forward and to truly live
I must be me, and myself I must forgive

it's done and it played out in that way
I can't describe my frame of mind
we've all made mistakes
I've re-lit the flame
that candle will stay alight again
it wasn't my finest hour
but now I'm not afraid to admit
it feels good to take back my power

but when you come to sleep at night
you can't escape your own thoughts
so think with intention
and live in your truth

lightning in the scars on her heart
still beating on and on

a promise to the stars
in her heart
sealed in blood

start the records
playing a new anthem
she's got the power

as a girl she escaped
into imagination dreams
but they have started to fade
and now the true sign
of her strength is
bringing them to life
before her eyes

I looked into his eyes
so dark and true
and saw not
the soul of a man
but a wolf
and I was not afraid
but intrigued

a song of heartbreak and transformation

making yourself into the person
who lives their dreams
is what makes life interesting

another spin of the wheel
another throw of the dice
another go at the game
another singer on another stage

you were a gardener with blue hands
while others grew flowers from the earth
you grew stars from the sky

sometimes she does
need to escape into her
own world for a while
but she's starting to learn
that the trick is bringing
her world to life
so she doesn't need to escape

hearing your story
at last, I feel like there's
someone like me
an anomaly
I felt so alone
when I was younger
now I realise while
I was thinking these thoughts
you were thinking them too
and that's an encouraging thought to think
that there's more rebels of thought out there

the words I say to myself
the music I play for myself
how beautiful I am
how rare my soul is
what I think of myself
is what matters most

is there anything more giving
than the process of transformation

navigate the world like a master
sail the seas like a commander
of your own soul
because if you don't
someone else will

dawn of legends
era of the courageous
age of rebels
generation of revolutionaries
aeon of luminaries
time of stoics
dance of glitches
song of anomalies
story of the free thinkers

as the journey goes on
I'll always remember
the sound of the midnight music
and all the moments it brought with it

a force of nature and of the stars
singing is the art of controlling the
sound energy in different forms
as the air erupts from your lungs
and vibrates through your vocal chords
you are the tuning fork,
the conductor of that frequency
no wonder we get moved to tears
at the sound of a nightingale's voice

once you've dipped your toes into the
beating heart stream of the cosmos
all you want to do is bathe in its starry light
forevermore, every night

she is a true virtuoso of poetry

I remember the words
to every song I have
written
so don't tell me
words have no power
when lyrics live
in my mind

a sea of thoughts you once brought to life
darling you hold the lightning bolt in your mind

it's always midnight in her heart

will you tell me the truth
about the music of your soul

I'm falling in love with the person I'm becoming

she is every song of powerful rising
she is every note of a hummingbird's whistle
she is every spark in a musician's heart
she is every tune in a little girl's imagination
she is every symphony of the orchestra
she is alive and luminescent with midnight music

a weaver of the energy of reality
bending the world to your will

breathe deep darling

imagine it's like an orchestra
you play the instrument in your soul
and then join with others
who know the same language
of music as you do
but they play a different instrument,
train and specialise in a different one
and it's the best of the best
the highest calibre
and we come together
to form an orchestra,
to play a song, a symphony
imagine the beautiful music
we could create then
the sounds we can create then
when we work together with others
who are on the same musical wavelength
who share the same dream

my soul feels better
when I'm vibrating
at higher frequencies

once you start transcending and transforming yourself
you realise nothing outside of you compares to that
feeling

in the midnight music
she transformed herself

in those moments
when the music
plays at midnight
I feel more myself
than ever

Elise x

Printed in Great Britain
by Amazon

28322863R00141